Sojourn

Flourishing on Earth, Yearning for Heaven

FAITHFUL LIVING, PART ONE

An Imprint of Precept®

Chattanooga

Published in the United States by

An Imprint of Precept®
PO Box 182218
Chattanooga, TN 37422

ISBN 978-1-63687-154-7

Copyright © 2023 by Yarrow™. All rights reserved.

Your purchase of this book enables Yarrow and Precept to fulfill our mission to engage people in relationship with God through knowing His Word. Thank you for purchasing an authorized copy of this book and for complying with copyright laws.

This material is published by and is the sole property of Yarrow of Chattanooga, Tennessee. No part of this publication may be reproduced, translated, or transmitted in any form or by any means, electronic or mechanical, including photocopying, recording, or any information storage and retrieval system, without permission in writing from the publisher.

For rights and permissions, please contact Yarrow at hello@yarrow.org.

Unless otherwise noted, all Scripture taken from ESV Bible (The Holy Bible, English Standard Version®). Copyright © 2001, 2007, 2011, 2016 by Crossway Books and Bibles, a Publishing Ministry of Good News Publishers.

Used by permission. All rights reserved.

First edition, September 2023
Printed in the United States of America

TABLE OF CONTENTS

Where we *are going*

Let's look ahead to where we are going. Below are the passages of Scripture we will be studying together to give us a full picture of faithful living as exiles.

06
Welcome

24
Chapter One
Self-Reflection #1
Setting the Stage

30
Chapter Two
The First Exiles
Genesis 3

40
Chapter Three
Summary
Genesis 3

84
Chapter Eight
An Exile in Action
Nehemiah 2

98
Chapter Nine
Summary
Nehemiah 1–2

104
Chapter Ten
Self-Reflection #2
Nehemiah 1–2

112
Chapter Eleven
Love Your City
Jeremiah 29

168
Chapter Sixteen
Summary
1 Peter 1–2

174
Chapter Seventeen
Wrap-up
How it Fits Together

180
Chapter Eighteen
Self-Reflection #3
Closing

46
Chapter Four
The Hall of Faith
Hebrews 11

58
Chapter Five
Strangers and Exiles
Hebrews 11

66
Chapter Six
Summary
Hebrews 11

72
Chapter Seven
A Faithful Exile
Nehemiah 1

126
Chapter Twelve
Summary
Jeremiah 29

132
Chapter Thirteen
Hope in Jesus
1 Peter 1

144
Chapter Fourteen
Faithful Living as Exiles
1 Peter 2

154
Chapter Fifteen
Joy in Suffering
1 Peter 1–2

INTRODUCTION

WEL-COME

> **If I find in myself a desire which no experience in this world can satisfy, the most probable explanation is that I was made for another world.** *C.S. Lewis*

Have you ever looked around and thought to yourself, *There must be something more?* Have you ever felt this desire that C.S. Lewis spoke of—a desire that nothing in this world can satisfy?

There is a longing in each one of us, an understanding that we were made for more than this world.

We were created for eternity and to be in perfect relationship with our Heavenly Father. And one day, this will be realized. We will see our God face to face. We will finally be "home," and He will satisfy our every longing.

But in the meantime, we are simply exiles in a world that is not our home. And with this exile comes some tension and a lot of questions.

How do we live as faithful Christians in this world in light of its culture? Do we isolate ourselves and try to recreate heaven on earth? Or do we learn to get comfortable here and take what we can get?

The goal of this Faithful Living study is to learn to live as faithful exiles here and now.

But what is *faithful living*? And what does it mean to be an *exile*?

INTRODUCTION

FAITHFUL LIVING

It can be easy to think of faithful living as a to-do list of behaviors and tasks to add to our lives or to avoid. But faithful living includes a change of perspective—a change of heart. It is about seeing this world through the eyes of God and adopting His perspective. It is about remembering our eternal home and our position as exiles here on this earth to change the way we live, think, act, and love, here and now.

EXILE

To be an exile consists of two main ideas: The first is a forced departure from home. The second is an inability to return home.

Refugees fleeing from war, persecution, or hardship are exiles. Heads of government might become exiles after a violent change in leadership forces them out of their country. Social exile can describe a fall from grace that keeps a person on the fringe of society. In each of these cases, the exiled person longs for their home, knowing full well they may never be able to return to it.

God's people have been exiled in various ways since the beginning of time. As Christians today, we continue to share in this condition as exiles. One day, we will return to the perfect relationship with God we were created for. But on this earth, we remain exiles, carrying with us the longing for our one true home.

Throughout this Faithful Living study, we will trace the thread of different exiles throughout the Bible. Along the way, we will see what Scripture teaches us about our position as exiles today and how faithful living can flow from there.

If you have questions or doubts, we hope you will bring them. If these concepts feel unfamiliar, that's okay too. We will continue to unpack them together through this study of the Bible.

We pray that your time in Scripture will pull you deeper into His presence and your relationship with Him. We pray that it will lead to lasting heart change that will forever affect the way you live, from the inside out.

WELCOME TO YARROW!

View a welcome video from one of our Yarrow team members by scanning this QR Code.

INTRODUCTION

What to **expect**

The old saying goes, "If you give a man a fish, you feed him for a day. If you teach a man to fish, you feed him for a lifetime." In other words, it's more important to know how to get a meal in the long run than to have one in hand today.

The Bible works the same way. Instead of giving you exact instructions for every circumstance, God gave you the Bible with big-picture truths about humanity, life, and Himself. The answers you seek aren't found in step-by-step instructions, but in knowing God. As your relationship with Him grows, so does your ability to see the world and your life through His eyes.

John talks about this in his Gospel:

Abide in me, and I in you. As the branch cannot bear fruit by itself, unless it abides in the vine, neither can you, unless you abide in me. I am the vine; you are the branches. Whoever abides in me and I in him, he it is that bears much fruit, for apart from me you can do nothing.

John 15:4–5

WHAT TO EXPECT

Scan the QR code to watch a video where we further explain what you can expect from this study.

The goal of this Bible study is not to give you a fish but to teach you how to fish. Basically, don't expect to be told what to believe. As we guide you through Scripture, you will develop the skills needed to approach the Bible on your own. We will leave room for you to take away what God has planned specifically for you.

Growing up in school, we focused on grades and scores, sometimes at the expense of authentic learning. We often bring that mindset to Bible studies. Here at Yarrow, we do Bible studies a little differently than you might be used to. We camp out in a passage for a while to let God speak through Scripture to our hearts and minds.

The questions we ask will not usually have a right or wrong answer. This might feel unfamiliar to you, and that's okay. This journey is designed to get you thinking critically about the text, the world, and your personal experiences. Studying this way allows us to absorb what the Holy Spirit is teaching us. Take your time. We'll help you make the connections, but it will be important that you rely on the Holy Spirit to guide you as well—not just us.

Over the next few weeks, we will go to Genesis, Hebrews, Nehemiah, Jeremiah, and 1 Peter to discover what it means to live as *faithful exiles here and now.* Along the way, we'll help you look for connections to your personal circumstances, and we'll guide you with reflection and discussion questions.

INTRODUCTION

How it works

Feel free to adapt it to your life, schedule, and relationships. Here's all we ask:

1. Choose two believers to talk to. We've seen that genuine transformation and growth often involve other people. Whether you're stumped, frustrated, or delighted by what you're discovering, it's important to have others walking with you. If you're meeting with a group, those people are automatically built in. If you're studying on your own, we encourage you to share with a believing spouse, friend, or mentor along the way.

2. Aim for consistency. Building routines that prioritize time in Scripture is an important part of setting yourself up for success. We encourage you to pick a time and place to go to the Bible every day, and then be flexible. If something happens and you miss a day (or a week), don't give up! This journey is about growth, not perfection.

The Method

We believe in a hands-on approach to Bible study. The Bible is thousands of years old, and it's easy to skim over strange stories or familiar verses without true understanding. To help you explore Scripture for yourself, we rely on the Precept Bible Study Method:

Observe: What does the text say?

Interpret: What does the text mean?

Apply: How should the meaning affect my life?

Taken together, these three components help you slow down, discover meaning, and find connections to your daily life.

THE METHOD:

01. Observe

The key to good observation is to slow down. This component in the process can feel a little tedious, but it's vital. Before you can jump to interpreting or applying Scripture, you must understand what is taking place in the text. Observation exercises will help bring clarity. The most common exercises include:

ANSWER THE 5WS AND AN H:

You'll answer straightforward questions like *who, what, when, where, why,* and *how* using what you read in a particular section of text. For example, you'll answer *when* with time phrases within the text like "the next day" or "in the morning." You'll find clues to *why* questions with words like "therefore" and "because" that explain more about what was just said. Doing this exercise helps you slow down and note the details of what you're reading so you don't miss anything. No special knowledge or insight is required.

MARKING:

To *mark* a word or phrase, you'll visually distinguish it with a shape or color. Once marked, you'll see at a glance where and how often the word or phrase appears. It's best to mark consistently and distinctively; that is, always mark the same word the same way and mark it differently than other words. Marking may also include making notes in the margins on comparisons, contrasts, or terms of conclusion. Marking may seem arbitrary at the moment, but it will help you pick up on themes and important points the author wants you to catch.

LISTING:

To *list* is to record all the details about something or someone in one place. These facts answer the 5Ws and an H questions. Then, you can review and reflect on everything you discover about a topic. This is most helpful when there is a lot of information scattered across several verses or chapters (for example, the miracles of Jesus or the story of creation).

THE METHOD:

02. Interpret

Once you're clear on what is being said in a text, you then need to know what it means. Thorough and careful observation flows into accurate interpretation. When you interpret Scripture, the context must be considered.

Scripture is a beautiful tapestry. When we observe a text (as outlined above), we focus on a small piece of the larger tapestry. We must also pay attention to the weave binding the material together. The context weaves throughout the entire biblical tapestry and binds it together.

To discover the context, we will pay attention to the historical and cultural context, the surrounding verses, the theme and structure of the entire book, other passages throughout the Bible on the same topic, and the overall story of redemption in Scripture. We may use the tools of cross-references or limited word studies to explore the meaning of a text. We'll ask you to look for key ideas or think about the meaning behind stories, parables, and poems. For example, it's one thing to know what Jesus said in a parable but another to understand what He meant.

Sometimes interpreting is straightforward with an obvious answer. Other times, it is more nuanced. Remember, we aren't going to tell you what to believe, so be patient with yourself. The Bible requires lifelong study, and the more you explore and meditate on Scripture, the more your understanding will grow.

THE METHOD:

03. Apply

Once you've seen what a text says and understood what it means, you need to consider how it affects your daily life. Sometimes a text will apply directly to something you can do or change externally, and sometimes it applies to matters of the heart or mind (and often, both)! We'll guide you with questions like:

- *What would change in your life if_____were true?*

- *How is your perspective on [current issue] affected by what you just read?*

- *What steps can you take this week to_____?*

Without application, Bible study is little more than an interesting academic exercise. This is where it's most important to have someone else involved. Christians need other Christians, and you'll find that your experience is richer and more enjoyable if you involve someone else in what you're learning.

01. **Observe**

02. **Interpret**

03. **Apply**

THE METHOD

Scan the QR Code to learn more about our Bible study method.

journal your thoughts

Let's spend a few moments thinking through this study's themes of exile and faithful living. Again, these concepts may feel new—and that's okay. Use the following pages to journal your thoughts as you reflect on the prompts below. Answer the questions as best as you can right now, knowing that we will return to them.

1.

Think about your position as an exile here on this earth. Have you ever thought about this before? What does this concept mean to you? How might your understanding of this impact your life?

2.

What does faithful living mean to you? How might living out your faith impact your life?

3.

What questions, if any, do you have coming into this study?

journal your thoughts

journal your thoughts

journal your thoughts

Go to God *in Prayer.*

Let's begin our time together in prayer. Throughout this study, we will end each day in prayer. Some days it will be a guided prayer, but most days you will write a personal prayer to God.

If this is new to you, please know there is no right or wrong way to do this. Your prayers do not need to be formatted in a certain way or use fancy language. Simply share your heart with God and direct your thoughts to Him.

Reflect on your answers from the previous page as you write your prayer to God. Tell Him how you feel as you begin this Faithful Living Series. Why does faithful living matter to you? How do you hope to be different by the end of this study? What questions do you have for Him? Write your prayer to Him below.

He is **near.**

He is **listening.**

And **He cares for you.**

CHAPTER ONE: SETTING THE STAGE

*Self-*Reflection *#1*

Let's begin with where you are. Take a moment to examine some struggles that may present themselves in your pursuit of faithful living. Faithful living is not about living perfectly, but rather living with a heart turned towards heaven and turned towards God and allowing this perspective to permeate every area of your life—your priorities, your habits, and how you spend your time. We invite you to be honest with yourself and with God. This is not meant to be a source of guilt or shame—these challenges exist for us all. But the first step to overcoming them is to acknowledge them.

Self-Reflection #1

1. **Circle any of the following struggles that get in the way of your faithful living:**

Control	Comparison	Time Management	Self-Image
Busyness	Technology	Laziness	Doubt
Comfort	Shame	Perfectionism	Loneliness
Lack of Trust	Social Media	Fear	Unforgiveness

   This is not a comprehensive list, so if other struggles exist for you, list them below.

2. **Let's take a moment to reflect on these.**

   Which struggles were you surprised to have circled?

   Reflect on each of the struggles you circled, one by one. Where do you see each one showing up in your life?

   How might the priorities and habits of your life begin to change by remembering your position as an exile on earth?

Praying in *Real-Life.*

As we journey through these next few weeks of Bible study, choose one of these struggles to keep in mind. Write it down in a journal or on a sheet of paper to remind yourself of it each day. We will return to it later, but for now, try to notice when it comes up. Notice how it affects your faithful living. And each time you do, take a moment to offer a prayer to God and ask for His help to overcome it. Remember to be kind and gracious to yourself along the way, as the Lord is kind and gracious to you.

Go to God *in Prayer.*

Father,

I confess that most days I do not live as faithfully as I want to.

I confess that I have sometimes allowed these struggles to stop me from living the life I long to live for You.

I invite You into these areas of my life.

Illuminate them for me, so I can learn to love You more and live with a heart turned toward heaven.

Help me remember that I am but an exile here, and show my heart what it truly longs for.

I give You permission to move in my heart and change me from the inside out.

Thank You for Your never-ending love and grace for me.

Amen.

CHAPTER TWO

The First Exiles

Genesis 3

> We are going to trace the thread of exiles throughout the Bible. As we reflect on their stories, we hope to understand how to live faithfully as exiles ourselves. Let's start at the beginning with the very first exiles.

EXILES IN SCRIPTURE

Scan the QR Code to learn more about the history of exiles in Scripture.

Let's begin with Genesis 3.

Read through Genesis 3 slowly, as if for the first time.

SCRIPTURE

Genesis 3

1. Now the serpent was more crafty than any other beast of the field that the LORD God had made. He said to the woman, "Did God actually say, 'You shall not eat of any tree in the garden'?"
2. And the woman said to the serpent, "We may eat of the fruit of the trees in the garden,
3. but God said, 'You shall not eat of the fruit of the tree that is in the midst of the garden, neither shall you touch it, lest you die.'"
4. But the serpent said to the woman, "You will not surely die.
5. For God knows that when you eat of it your eyes will be opened, and you will be like God, knowing good and evil."
6. So when the woman saw that the tree was good for food, and that it was a delight to the eyes, and that the tree was to be desired to make one wise, she took of its fruit and ate, and she also gave some to her husband who was with her, and he ate.
7. Then the eyes of both were opened, and they knew that they were naked. And they sewed fig leaves together and made themselves loincloths.
8. And they heard the sound of the LORD God walking in the garden in the cool of the day, and the man and his wife hid themselves from the presence of the LORD God among the trees of the garden.
9. But the LORD God called to the man and said to him, "Where are you?"
10. And he said, "I heard the sound of you in the garden, and I was afraid, because I was naked, and I hid myself."
11. He said, "Who told you that you were naked? Have you eaten of the tree of which I commanded you not to eat?"
12. The man said, "The woman whom you gave to be with me, she gave me fruit of the tree, and I ate."
13. Then the LORD God said to the woman, "What is this that you have done?" The woman said, "The serpent deceived me, and I ate."

14   The LORD God said to the serpent,

> "Because you have done this,
>> cursed are you above all livestock
>> and above all beasts of the field;
>
> on your belly you shall go,
>> and dust you shall eat
>
> all the days of your life.

15   I will put enmity between you and the woman,
>> and between your offspring and her offspring;
>
> he shall bruise your head,
>> and you shall bruise his heel."

16   To the woman he said,

> "I will surely multiply your pain in childbearing;
>> in pain you shall bring forth children.
>
> Your desire shall be contrary to your husband,
>> but he shall rule over you."

17   And to Adam he said,

> "Because you have listened to the voice of your wife
>> and have eaten of the tree
>
> of which I commanded you,
>> 'You shall not eat of it,'
>
> cursed is the ground because of you;
>> in pain you shall eat of it all the days of your life;

18   thorns and thistles it shall bring forth for you;
>> and you shall eat the plants of the field.

19   By the sweat of your face
> you shall eat bread,
>
> till you return to the ground,
>> for out of it you were taken;
>
> for you are dust,
>> and to dust you shall return."

SCRIPTURE

20 The man called his wife's name Eve, because she was the mother of all living.
21 And the LORD God made for Adam and for his wife garments of skins and clothed them.
22 Then the LORD God said, "Behold, the man has become like one of us in knowing good and evil. Now, lest he reach out his hand and take also of the tree of life and eat, and live forever—"
23 therefore the LORD God sent him out from the garden of Eden to work the ground from which he was taken.
24 He drove out the man, and at the east of the garden of Eden he placed the cherubim and a flaming sword that turned every way to guard the way to the tree of life.

LET'S TAKE A CLOSER LOOK...

1. ─────────────

How did Adam and Eve's desires lead them to disobey God by eating the forbidden fruit? What does this say about their trust in God?

2. ─────────────

After Adam and Eve sinned, what did God do next? What does God's pursuit of Adam and Eve reveal about His desires for them?

3. ─────────────

List below the consequences God gave to Adam and Eve for their sin in verses 16–24 and to whom each consequence was given.

- verse 16:

- verses 17–19:

- verses 23–24:

LET'S TAKE A CLOSER LOOK...

4.

Notice the last consequence God gave in verses 23–24 where we see Adam and Eve become the first exiles.

Looking at these verses, how were Adam and Eve exiled?

How were their lives different after God exiled them from the garden?

5.

Reflecting on Adam and Eve's exile from the Garden of Eden, how have you also been exiled?
Note: We will continue to trace this theme through every passage of Scripture we read, so if it feels hard to make the connections right now, that's okay! We will keep coming back to it.

Go to God *in Prayer.*

Before we finish our time in Genesis 3, let's take a moment to thank God for His Word. What truths did God reveal to you in your exploration of Genesis 3 today? What questions do you still have for Him? What do you hope to remember and carry with you throughout your day? Write your prayer to God below.

CHAPTER THREE

Summary

Genesis 3

Spend time slowing down and reflecting on all you have discovered from Genesis 3 by filling out the summary chart on the next page.

If there are some questions that you are unable to answer today, that's okay. We will practice this at the end of each passage of Scripture. A question that is hard today may become clearer as you go on. At the end of the study, we will look at all the charts together to see the Bible as one full story and how our own stories intersect with God's story.

GENESIS 3 SUMMARY CHART

Theme/Big Idea

What did you learn about God/Jesus?

What did you learn about yourself?

What did you learn about living in exile?

What did you learn about faithful living?

Personal Takeaway

Faithful Exile

Go to God *in Prayer.*

Let's pray. These summary chapters are shorter. Use the extra time and space you have today to sit with the Lord. Thank God for all He has begun to teach you throughout your exploration of Genesis 3. Tell Him anything that is on your heart, and ask Him any questions that may still be on your mind. Write your prayer to Him below.

CHAPTER FOUR

The Hall of Faith

Hebrews 11

Let's continue to follow the thread of God's people as exiles with Hebrews 11.

CONTEXT

Hebrews is one of the New Testament epistles. An epistle is a letter written to a specific church, group, or individual learning to follow Christ. This letter was written to the Hebrews to encourage the Jewish members of the Church during a time of strong persecution. Although Hebrews is a New Testament book, this chapter will recount the stories of many faithful men and women from the Old Testament.

Scan the QR Code to learn more about the context of the book of Hebrews.

Let's begin with observation.

Read through Hebrews 11 and take note of the key word that is repeated throughout the chapter. Underline this word or mark it with the same color each time you see it appear.

Hebrews 11

1. Now faith is the assurance of things hoped for, the conviction of things not seen.
2. For by it the people of old received their commendation.
3. By faith we understand that the universe was created by the word of God, so that what is seen was not made out of things that are visible.
4. By faith Abel offered to God a more acceptable sacrifice than Cain, through which he was commended as righteous, God commending him by accepting his gifts. And through his faith, though he died, he still speaks.
5. By faith Enoch was taken up so that he should not see death, and he was not found, because God had taken him. Now before he was taken he was commended as having pleased God.
6. And without faith it is impossible to please him, for whoever would draw near to God must believe that he exists and that he rewards those who seek him.
7. By faith Noah, being warned by God concerning events as yet unseen, in reverent fear constructed an ark for the saving of his household. By this he condemned the world and became an heir of the righteousness that comes by faith.
8. By faith Abraham obeyed when he was called to go out to a place that he was to receive as an inheritance. And he went out, not knowing where he was going.
9. By faith he went to live in the land of promise, as in a foreign land, living in tents with Isaac and Jacob, heirs with him of the same promise.
10. For he was looking forward to the city that has foundations, whose designer and builder is God.
11. By faith Sarah herself received power to conceive, even when she was past the age, since she considered him faithful who had promised.

12 Therefore from one man, and him as good as dead, were born descendants as many as the stars of heaven and as many as the innumerable grains of sand by the seashore.

13 These all died in faith, not having received the things promised, but having seen them and greeted them from afar, and having acknowledged that they were strangers and exiles on the earth.

14 For people who speak thus make it clear that they are seeking a homeland.

15 If they had been thinking of that land from which they had gone out, they would have had opportunity to return.

16 But as it is, they desire a better country, that is, a heavenly one. Therefore God is not ashamed to be called their God, for he has prepared for them a city.

17 By faith Abraham, when he was tested, offered up Isaac, and he who had received the promises was in the act of offering up his only son,

18 of whom it was said, "Through Isaac shall your offspring be named."

19 He considered that God was able even to raise him from the dead, from which, figuratively speaking, he did receive him back.

20 By faith Isaac invoked future blessings on Jacob and Esau.

21 By faith Jacob, when dying, blessed each of the sons of Joseph, bowing in worship over the head of his staff.

22 By faith Joseph, at the end of his life, made mention of the exodus of the Israelites and gave directions concerning his bones.

23 By faith Moses, when he was born, was hidden for three months by his parents, because they saw that the child was beautiful, and they were not afraid of the king's edict.

24 By faith Moses, when he was grown up, refused to be called the son of Pharaoh's daughter,

25 choosing rather to be mistreated with the people of God than to enjoy the fleeting pleasures of sin.

26 He considered the reproach of Christ greater wealth than the treasures of Egypt, for he was looking to the reward.

SCRIPTURE

27 By faith he left Egypt, not being afraid of the anger of the king, for he endured as seeing him who is invisible.

28 By faith he kept the Passover and sprinkled the blood, so that the Destroyer of the firstborn might not touch them.

29 By faith the people crossed the Red Sea as on dry land, but the Egyptians, when they attempted to do the same, were drowned.

30 By faith the walls of Jericho fell down after they had been encircled for seven days.

31 By faith Rahab the prostitute did not perish with those who were disobedient, because she had given a friendly welcome to the spies.

32 And what more shall I say? For time would fail me to tell of Gideon, Barak, Samson, Jephthah, of David and Samuel and the prophets—

33 who through faith conquered kingdoms, enforced justice, obtained promises, stopped the mouths of lions,

34 quenched the power of fire, escaped the edge of the sword, were made strong out of weakness, became mighty in war, put foreign armies to flight.

35 Women received back their dead by resurrection. Some were tortured, refusing to accept release, so that they might rise again to a better life.

36 Others suffered mocking and flogging, and even chains and imprisonment.

37 They were stoned, they were sawn in two, they were killed with the sword. They went about in skins of sheep and goats, destitute, afflicted, mistreated—

38 of whom the world was not worthy—wandering about in deserts and mountains, and in dens and caves of the earth.

39 And all these, though commended through their faith, did not receive what was promised,

40 since God had provided something better for us, that apart from us they should not be made perfect.

LET'S OBSERVE THE TEXT.

1. _____

What is the key word that is repeated throughout this chapter?

2. _____

How does the author of Hebrews define faith in verse 1?

3. _____

Paraphrase this verse in your own words.

4.

Look at verse 6. According to the author of Hebrews, why does our faith matter to God?

5.

How can your insights on faith from Hebrews 11 inform your own faithful living?

LET'S TAKE A CLOSER LOOK...

Let's take a closer look at some of these men and women of faith. Fill in the second column below with their acts of faith as mentioned in Hebrews 11.

Name	Acts of Faith	One Word Summary
Abel	Offered to God an acceptable sacrifice	Obedience
Noah		
Abraham		
Sarah		
Moses		
Rahab		

Now, fill in the last column with the word from the list below that you feel best summarizes each act of faith:

- Obedience
- Worship
- Sacrifice
- Belief

Reflect *and apply.*

Choosing one of the four words from the previous page, think about one practical thing that you can do today as an act of faith in God. Write it down below and commit to doing it by the end of the day. Remember that a lifestyle devoted to God is not simply about a behavior or an action. God desires our hearts. Commit to this action or attitude wholeheartedly out of genuine love for your Father.

Go to God *in Prayer.*

We will return to Hebrews 11 tomorrow. But before we close out today, let's take a moment to thank God for the examples of these faithful men and women and offer our hearts to Him in prayer. What stood out to you today? What truths did you learn about faith? In what ways would you like to ask God to help you in your pursuit of adopting His perspective? Write your prayer to Him below.

CHAPTER FIVE

Strangers and Exiles

Hebrews 11

> Now that we have looked at what these godly men and women were able to do by faith, let's look at *how* they were able to do what they did.

Let's focus on Hebrews 11:13–16.

Read through verses 13–16 slowly once more. Answer the questions on the following pages. These are our key verses for this chapter.

Hebrews 11:13–16

13 These all died in faith, not having received the things promised, but having seen them and greeted them from afar, and having acknowledged that they were strangers and exiles on the earth.

14 For people who speak thus make it clear that they are seeking a homeland.

15 If they had been thinking of that land from which they had gone out, they would have had opportunity to return.

16 But as it is, they desire a better country, that is, a heavenly one. Therefore God is not ashamed to be called their God, for he has prepared for them a city.

1.

In verses 13–16, these men and women are called "strangers and exiles . . . seeking a homeland." What homeland were they longing for?

2.

How does their position and perspective as "strangers and exiles" relate to your own?

3.

How would your character and life change if you adopted this same heavenly perspective?

4. Has your understanding of faithful living evolved in light of what you have studied today? If yes, how?

5. What is one practical way you can incorporate this new perspective into your real-world life?

THEY WERE

strangers and exiles

ON THE EARTH

Go to God *in Prayer.*

Before we close out our time in Hebrews 11, let's pause and pray. Take a look at your answer to the last question and share this plan with God. Share with Him your desire and your commitment to faithful living. Confess to Him your weakness and your need for Him and His help. Invite Him into this pursuit. Write your prayer to God below.

CHAPTER SIX

Summary

Hebrews 11

Spend time slowing down and reflecting on all you have discovered from Hebrews 11 by filling out the summary chart on the next page.

If there are some questions that you are unable to answer today, that's okay. We will practice this at the end of each passage of Scripture. A question that is hard today may become clearer as you go on. At the end of the study, we will look at all the charts together to see the Bible as one full story and how our own stories intersect with God's story.

HEBREWS 11 SUMMARY CHART

Theme/Big Idea

What did you learn about God/Jesus?

What did you learn about yourself?

What did you learn about living in exile?

What did you learn about faithful living?

Personal Takeaway

FAITHFUL LIVING, PART ONE

Now **faith** *is the assurance of things* **hoped for,** *the conviction of things* **not seen.**

Hebrews 11:1

Go to God *in Prayer.*

Let's close our time together in prayer. Come before God, thanking Him for all He is teaching you and all the ways He inspires you through the study of Scripture. Share with Him anything that is on your mind and in your heart. Write your prayer to Him below.

CHAPTER SEVEN

A Faithful Exile

Nehemiah 1

> Let's look to Nehemiah for an example of an exile who lived with a heart turned toward God during his time. It is worth noting as we delve into a case study with Nehemiah, that while he was certainly a faithful man of God with many helpful things to teach us, he was also human—flawed and sinful. Let's keep this in mind, remembering that the only person we seek to fully emulate is Jesus.

CONTEXT

Nehemiah is a historical book of the Old Testament. It takes place after the Babylonians have destroyed Jerusalem and its temple and taken many of God's people into exile to Babylon. When Nehemiah's story begins during the Exile, some Israelites have already begun to return to Jerusalem to rebuild both their city and their lives. They have successfully rebuilt the temple, but as we will read together in Nehemiah 1, the city walls are still in ruins, a source of great trouble and shame for the Israelites.

Scan the QR Code to learn more about the context of the book of Nehemiah.

Let's begin with observation.

Read Nehemiah 1 and mark each of the following words or phrases distinctively (underline, box, circle, or use separate colors to highlight):

- *When?* (Look for specific and general time markers, like *the month of Chislev* and *soon*, and mark them all the same way.)

- *Where?* (Look for specific and general locations, like *Jerusalem* and *heaven*, and mark them all the same way.)

- *God* and His synonyms and pronouns *(God of heaven, you, your, etc.)*

Here are some marking suggestions:

1. *"Now it happened in the* month of Chislev*"*

2. *"The wall of Jerusalem is broken down . . ."*

3. *". . . I continued fasting and praying before the God of heaven"*

Nehemiah 1

1 The words of Nehemiah the son of Hacaliah. Now it happened in the month of Chislev, in the twentieth year, as I was in Susa the citadel,

2 that Hanani, one of my brothers, came with certain men from Judah. And I asked them concerning the Jews who escaped, who had survived the exile, and concerning Jerusalem.

3 And they said to me, "The remnant there in the province who had survived the exile is in great trouble and shame. The wall of Jerusalem is broken down, and its gates are destroyed by fire."

4 As soon as I heard these words I sat down and wept and mourned for days, and I continued fasting and praying before the God of heaven.

5 And I said, "O LORD God of heaven, the great and awesome God who keeps covenant and steadfast love with those who love him and keep his commandments,

6 let your ear be attentive and your eyes open, to hear the prayer of your servant that I now pray before you day and night for the people of Israel your servants, confessing the sins of the people of Israel, which we have sinned against you. Even I and my father's house have sinned.

7 We have acted very corruptly against you and have not kept the commandments, the statutes, and the rules that you commanded your servant Moses.

8 Remember the word that you commanded your servant Moses, saying, 'If you are unfaithful, I will scatter you among the peoples,

9 but if you return to me and keep my commandments and do them, though your outcasts are in the uttermost parts of heaven, from there I will gather them and bring them to the place that I have chosen, to make my name dwell there.'

SCRIPTURE

10   They are your servants and your people, whom you have redeemed by your great power and by your strong hand.
11   O Lord, let your ear be attentive to the prayer of your servant, and to the prayer of your servants who delight to fear your name, and give success to your servant today, and grant him mercy in the sight of this man."
  Now I was cupbearer to the king.

LET'S TAKE A CLOSER LOOK...

Let's begin by looking at 1:3–4.

1.

What news does Nehemiah receive in verse 3?

2.

How does Nehemiah respond to this news in verse 4? Be specific.

3.

What can you learn from the way Nehemiah responds, specifically, the order in which he does so?

Let's move to verses 5–11 where we see how Nehemiah's heart for his people and his ancestral homeland moves him to honest and thoughtful prayer.

Note: As a reminder, the Bible is one whole and complete story, so keep in mind what you learned in Hebrews 11 as you work through these questions.

4.

Look to where you marked God throughout Nehemiah's prayer. What does Nehemiah's prayer show us about how he views God, and the relationship Nehemiah has with Him?

5.

What does his prayer continue to show us about his heart for his people and his ancestral homeland?

6.

When you think about your position as an exile on this earth, how do you relate to Nehemiah's position as an exile and the heart that he has for his homeland?

7.

How can we adopt Nehemiah's heart for God's people and His kingdom?

8.

How would this change the way you live faithfully here and now?

Go to God *in Prayer.*

As we close out our time in Nehemiah 1 today, let's turn our hearts toward God and heaven. Ask God to deepen your love for His people and His heavenly kingdom. How do you hope the way you live here and now on this earth will be changed? Lift your heart, desires, and hopes to Him. Write your prayer to Him below.

CHAPTER EIGHT

An Exile in Action

Nehemiah 2

We saw in Nehemiah 1 that Nehemiah was a man with a great heart and love for his people and his homeland, which led him from weeping and mourning to honest prayer. In Nehemiah 2, Nehemiah's heart leads him beyond thought and prayer into action.

Let's begin with observation.

We are introduced to some new people in this chapter. Read chapter 2 and mark references to:

1. *King Artaxerxes* and synonyms and pronouns for him

2. *Sanballat the Horonite, Tobiah the Ammonite,* and *Geshem the Arab*

Here are some marking suggestions:

1. "... in the twentieth year of King Artaxerxes..."

2. "But when Sanballat the Horonite and Tobiah the Ammonite servant and Geshem the Arab heard..."

Nehemiah 2

1. In the month of Nisan, in the twentieth year of King Artaxerxes, when wine was before him, I took up the wine and gave it to the king. Now I had not been sad in his presence.

2. And the king said to me, "Why is your face sad, seeing you are not sick? This is nothing but sadness of the heart." Then I was very much afraid.

3. I said to the king, "Let the king live forever! Why should not my face be sad, when the city, the place of my fathers' graves, lies in ruins, and its gates have been destroyed by fire?"

4. Then the king said to me, "What are you requesting?" So I prayed to the God of heaven.

5. And I said to the king, "If it pleases the king, and if your servant has found favor in your sight, that you send me to Judah, to the city of my fathers' graves, that I may rebuild it."

6. And the king said to me (the queen sitting beside him), "How long will you be gone, and when will you return?" So it pleased the king to send me when I had given him a time.

7. And I said to the king, "If it pleases the king, let letters be given me to the governors of the province Beyond the River, that they may let me pass through until I come to Judah,

8. and a letter to Asaph, the keeper of the king's forest, that he may give me timber to make beams for the gates of the fortress of the temple, and for the wall of the city, and for the house that I shall occupy." And the king granted me what I asked, for the good hand of my God was upon me.

9. Then I came to the governors of the province Beyond the River and gave them the king's letters. Now the king had sent with me officers of the army and horsemen.

10. But when Sanballat the Horonite and Tobiah the Ammonite servant heard this, it displeased them greatly that someone had come to seek the welfare of the people of Israel.

11 So I went to Jerusalem and was there three days.
12 Then I arose in the night, I and a few men with me. And I told no one what my God had put into my heart to do for Jerusalem. There was no animal with me but the one on which I rode.
13 I went out by night by the Valley Gate to the Dragon Spring and to the Dung Gate, and I inspected the walls of Jerusalem that were broken down and its gates that had been destroyed by fire.
14 Then I went on to the Fountain Gate and to the King's Pool, but there was no room for the animal that was under me to pass.
15 Then I went up in the night by the valley and inspected the wall, and I turned back and entered by the Valley Gate, and so returned.
16 And the officials did not know where I had gone or what I was doing, and I had not yet told the Jews, the priests, the nobles, the officials, and the rest who were to do the work.
17 Then I said to them, "You see the trouble we are in, how Jerusalem lies in ruins with its gates burned. Come, let us build the wall of Jerusalem, that we may no longer suffer derision."
18 And I told them of the hand of my God that had been upon me for good, and also of the words that the king had spoken to me. And they said, "Let us rise up and build." So they strengthened their hands for the good work.
19 But when Sanballat the Horonite and Tobiah the Ammonite servant and Geshem the Arab heard of it, they jeered at us and despised us and said, "What is this thing that you are doing? Are you rebelling against the king?"
20 Then I replied to them, "The God of heaven will make us prosper, and we his servants will arise and build, but you have no portion or right or claim in Jerusalem."

LET'S TAKE A CLOSER LOOK...

1. ───────────

What is Nehemiah's expression before the king in 2:1–2?

2. ───────────

What does this continue to show us about Nehemiah's heart for his people and his homeland?

3. ───────────

In verse 4, what does Nehemiah do immediately after King Artaxerxes asks for his request?

4. What does this continue to show us about Nehemiah's relationship with God?

5. List below Nehemiah's requests to the king in verses 5–8. This is the first part of his action plan.

6. Why does King Artaxerxes grant Nehemiah's request?

7. _____

After traveling to and arriving in Jerusalem, we see the second part of Nehemiah's action plan taking place in verses 13–16. What does Nehemiah do in these verses?

8. _____

Finally, in verses 17–18, Nehemiah shares his plan with others. What does he say? How do they respond to his plan?

> "Let us rise up and build."
>
> Nehemiah 2:18

Reflect *and apply.*

1.

Why is it essential to have a prayerful and thought-out action plan for faithful living in your own life?

2.

Look where you marked Sanballat the Horonite, Tobiah the Ammonite, and Geshem the Arab. In these verses, we see the first example of opposition against Nehemiah's plan. Look back to page 26 at the struggle you face in your own pursuit of faithful living. Using the struggle you chose to keep in mind throughout this study, create an action plan on the next page to help you overcome it. Nehemiah had a detailed plan. Try to do the same with yours.

Here are some things you can think through:

- *What* will you do?
- *How* will you do it?
- *When/where* will you do it?
- *Who* can do it with you or hold you accountable?
- *Why* are you doing it?

Struggle	Plan

Go to God *in Prayer.*

As we close out our time in Nehemiah, let's take a moment to turn our hearts toward God and heaven. Ask God to deepen your longing for your eternal home. In doing so, how do you hope that the way you live will be changed here and now on this earth? Lift your heart and desires and hopes to Him. Write your prayer to Him below.

CHAPTER NINE

Summary

Nehemiah 1–2

Spend time slowing down and reflecting on all you have discovered from Nehemiah 1–2 by filling out the summary chart on the next page.

If there are some questions that you are unable to answer today, that's okay. We will practice this at the end of each passage of Scripture. A question that is hard today may become clearer as you go on. At the end of the study, we will look at all the charts together to see the Bible as one full story and how our own stories intersect with God's story.

NEHEMIAH 1–2 SUMMARY CHART

Theme/Big Idea

What did you learn about God/Jesus?

What did you learn about yourself?

What did you learn about living in exile?

What did you learn about faithful living?

Personal Takeaway

Go to God *in Prayer.*

Let's return to the Lord in prayer. Thank God for Nehemiah's bold and faithful example. Ask Him for anything you need as you continue in this journey of living with a heart turned toward heaven. Write your prayer to Him below.

CHAPTER TEN

Self-Reflection #2

> As we close out our time in Nehemiah, let's take a moment to retrace the thread we have been following and reflect on what we have discovered.

Self-Reflection #2

In Genesis, we saw how sin and disobedience led us into the first exile. We were created for perfect union with God in Eden, and our hearts continue to long for this even as we live as exiles on this earth. In Hebrews, we read a long list of faithful men and women who lived in light of this truth with their heavenly home in their hearts. And in Nehemiah, we read about an exile who lived faithfully with a deep passion for his people. He devised an action plan to serve and restore them, despite any opposition coming his way.

1.

As you look back on the struggle you chose to focus on at the beginning of this study, have you seen any changes in yourself? If so, explain below. If not, what changes would you still like to see, and what are some steps you can take to get there?

2.

Look back on the first few questions you answered on page 26 as well as to the summary charts on pages 42, 68, and 100 you have filled out. Has your understanding of your position as an exile on earth grown? If so, how?

3.

In light of all we have studied about your position as an exile on this earth, how do you currently understand living life from God's perspective?

Go to God *in Prayer.*

Father,

Thank You for this journey that we are on together.

Thank You for walking with me every step of the way.

I praise You and give You glory for all You have already done
in me and through me.

Help me remember that I am but an exile on this earth,
longing to walk with You in perfect relationship for all of eternity.

And until that day comes,
teach me to walk faithfully with You here and now.

Amen.

Take a step *in community.*

After you have self-reflected and talked with God, take an opportunity to *talk with someone else.* Choose 1–3 people you trust and share with them what you have been learning and processing. Share with them the ways you have already seen God begin to change you and where you would still like to go. Also, share with them your action plan to overcome any struggle as you continue to pursue faithful living. Then, ask them to check in and hold you accountable as they walk the rest of this journey with you.

Not sure what to say? You can start like this:

I've been working through my Bible study on Faithful Living. I've been learning _____, and I'm already beginning to see God change me in these ways: _____ . I still have some chapters to go. By the end of this, I'm hoping that _____ .

What do you think about these things?

Will you walk with me and pray with me through the rest of this study?

CHAPTER ELEVEN

Love Your City

Jeremiah 29:1–14

So far, we have sought to understand our position as exiles on this earth and to adopt God's perspective. We know this world is not our home and that we are awaiting our homecoming in heaven. But until then, how can we love, serve, and invest in our communities here and now? We have seen Nehemiah's great heart for his people. Now let's look to Jeremiah to learn more.

CONTEXT

The book of Jeremiah is a prophetic book of the Old Testament. God called the prophet Jeremiah to predict the destruction of Jerusalem at the hands of Babylon. The Babylonians captured and exiled the Israelites—the same exile in which the book of Nehemiah is set. However, the book of Jeremiah takes place many years before Nehemiah. Jeremiah is set in the years leading up to and within the early years of the exile.

Scan the QR code to learn more about the context of the book of Jeremiah.

Let's begin with observation.

Read through Jeremiah 29:1–14.

Jeremiah 29:1–14

1 These are the words of the letter that Jeremiah the prophet sent from Jerusalem to the surviving elders of the exiles, and to the priests, the prophets, and all the people, whom Nebuchadnezzar had taken into exile from Jerusalem to Babylon.

2 This was after King Jeconiah and the queen mother, the eunuchs, the officials of Judah and Jerusalem, the craftsmen, and the metal workers had departed from Jerusalem.

3 The letter was sent by the hand of Elasah the son of Shaphan and Gemariah the son of Hilkiah, whom Zedekiah king of Judah sent to Babylon to Nebuchadnezzar king of Babylon. It said:

4 "Thus says the LORD of hosts, the God of Israel, to all the exiles whom I have sent into exile from Jerusalem to Babylon:

5 Build houses and live in them; plant gardens and eat their produce.

6 Take wives and have sons and daughters; take wives for your sons, and give your daughters in marriage, that they may bear sons and daughters; multiply there, and do not decrease.

7 But seek the welfare of the city where I have sent you into exile, and pray to the LORD on its behalf, for in its welfare you will find your welfare.

8 For thus says the LORD of hosts, the God of Israel: Do not let your prophets and your diviners who are among you deceive you, and do not listen to the dreams that they dream,

9 for it is a lie that they are prophesying to you in my name; I did not send them, declares the LORD.

10 "For thus says the LORD: When seventy years are completed for Babylon, I will visit you, and I will fulfill to you my promise and bring you back to this place.

11 For I know the plans I have for you, declares the Lord, plans for welfare and not for evil, to give you a future and a hope.

12 Then you will call upon me and come and pray to me, and I will hear you.

SCRIPTURE

13 You will seek me and find me, when you seek me with all your heart.
14 I will be found by you, declares the LORD, and I will restore your fortunes and gather you from all the nations and all the places where I have driven you, declares the LORD, and I will bring you back to the place from which I sent you into exile.

Let's begin with observation.

1.

Looking at the context in verse 1, who is the author of this letter?

2.

Who is he writing to and what is their situation?

3.

List below the commands God gave the exiles in verses 4–7.

4.
   List below the promises God gave the exiles in verses 10–14.

5.
   In your own words, what is God asking of the Israelite exiles?

LET'S TAKE A CLOSER LOOK...

In verse 7, God promises the Israelite exiles that "in [the city's] welfare you will find your welfare."

Note: The word "welfare" here means the good health, happiness, wholeness, and peace of a group of people.

1. Knowing that God is not asking us to be selfishly motivated, what do you think He means by this? How would investing in your city's flourishing bring about your own?

2. If God promised to bring the Israelite exiles home after 70 years, why do you think it matters to Him that they "seek the welfare of the city"? Why should they invest in a community that is not their permanent homeland? What does this show us about the heart of God and what is important to Him?

3.

In what ways can you choose to love, serve, and invest in your community, knowing that you too are an exile here, awaiting your eternal home?

Go to God *in Prayer.*

Following God's invitation in verse 7 to *"pray to the Lord on its behalf,"* write a prayer to God for your city. Thank Him for placing you exactly where you are on purpose. Place the needs of your city before Him. Ask Him for the things that you believe will make your city thrive, remembering that *"in its welfare, you will find your welfare."*

Reflect *and apply.*

We hope that studying the Bible will always move us beyond knowledge to action, not simply to read the words of Scripture but to allow it to change us from the inside out. Take time this week to learn more about the city where God has placed you and commit to serving and investing in it. Here are some ideas to help you get started:

- Learn who your city mayor and officials are and write them a note of gratitude.

- Write a note expressing any concerns, thoughts, or ideas about your city to your mayor and city officials.

- Find out what local events or activities are happening in your city and the ways to get involved.

- Commit to volunteering around your city.

- Shop locally.

- Meet your neighbors.

- Pray for your city.

CHAPTER TWELVE

Summary

Jeremiah 29

Spend time slowing down and reflecting on all you have discovered from Jeremiah 29 by filling out the summary chart on the next page.

If there are some questions that you are unable to answer today, that's okay. We will practice this at the end of each passage of Scripture. A question that is hard today may become clearer as you go on. At the end of the study, we will look at all the charts together to see the Bible as one full story and how our own stories intersect with God's story.

JEREMIAH 29 SUMMARY CHART

Theme/Big Idea

What did you learn about God/Jesus?

What did you learn about yourself?

What did you learn about living in exile?

What did you learn about faithful living?

Personal Takeaway

> *You will seek me and* **find me,** *when you seek me with* **all your heart.**
>
> Jeremiah 29:13

Go to God *in Prayer.*

Come before God in prayer. Thank Him for what He has taught you through your exploration of Jeremiah 29 and for the ways that it inspires you to action. Ask Him for the courage and compassion to love and serve your city and its people. Continue praying for your city. Share with God all that is on your heart, and ask Him for anything you might need today. Write your prayer to Him below.

CHAPTER THIRTEEN

Hope in Jesus

1 Peter 1

> We have looked at several examples of exiles throughout the Old Testament. Let's look to 1 Peter to see an example of some exiles who lived in the first century and learn about faithful living in light of Jesus.

CONTEXT OF 1 PETER

Scan the QR code to learn more about the context of the book of 1 Peter.

Let's begin with observation.

Read once through 1 Peter 1. As you do, mark each mention of *Jesus Christ* (and any synonyms and pronouns for Him) with a cross. Make a note of anything that immediately stands out to you below.

1 Peter 1

1 Peter, an apostle of Jesus Christ,
To those who are elect exiles of the Dispersion in Pontus, Galatia, Cappadocia, Asia, and Bithynia,

2 according to the foreknowledge of God the Father, in the sanctification of the Spirit, for obedience to Jesus Christ and for sprinkling with his blood: May grace and peace be multiplied to you.

3 Blessed be the God and Father of our Lord Jesus Christ! According to his great mercy, he has caused us to be born again to a living hope through the resurrection of Jesus Christ from the dead,

4 to an inheritance that is imperishable, undefiled, and unfading, kept in heaven for you,

5 who by God's power are being guarded through faith for a salvation ready to be revealed in the last time.

6 In this you rejoice, though now for a little while, if necessary, you have been grieved by various trials,

7 so that the tested genuineness of your faith—more precious than gold that perishes though it is tested by fire—may be found to result in praise and glory and honor at the revelation of Jesus Christ.

8 Though you have not seen him, you love him. Though you do not now see him, you believe in him and rejoice with joy that is inexpressible and filled with glory,

9 obtaining the outcome of your faith, the salvation of your souls.

10 Concerning this salvation, the prophets who prophesied about the grace that was to be yours searched and inquired carefully,

11 inquiring what person or time the Spirit of Christ in them was indicating when he predicted the sufferings of Christ and the subsequent glories.

12 It was revealed to them that they were serving not themselves but you, in the things that have now been announced to you through those who preached the good news to you by the Holy Spirit sent from heaven, things into which angels long to look.

13 Therefore, preparing your minds for action, and being sober-minded, set your hope fully on the grace that will be brought to you at the revelation of Jesus Christ.
14 As obedient children, do not be conformed to the passions of your former ignorance,
15 but as he who called you is holy, you also be holy in all your conduct,
16 since it is written, "You shall be holy, for I am holy."
17 And if you call on him as Father who judges impartially according to each one's deeds, conduct yourselves with fear throughout the time of your exile,
18 knowing that you were ransomed from the futile ways inherited from your forefathers, not with perishable things such as silver or gold,
19 but with the precious blood of Christ, like that of a lamb without blemish or spot.
20 He was foreknown before the foundation of the world but was made manifest in the last times for the sake of you
21 who through him are believers in God, who raised him from the dead and gave him glory, so that your faith and hope are in God.
22 Having purified your souls by your obedience to the truth for a sincere brotherly love, love one another earnestly from a pure heart,
23 since you have been born again, not of perishable seed but of imperishable, through the living and abiding word of God;
24 for

> "All flesh is like grass
>   and all its glory like the flower of grass.
> The grass withers,
>   and the flower falls,

25   but the word of the Lord remains forever."

And this word is the good news that was preached to you.

LET'S OBSERVE THE TEXT.

1.

Let's begin with the context in 1:1.

- Who is the author of this letter?

- Who is he writing it to?

2.

Reread verses 1–12. Summarize Peter's main message to the exiles in these verses in one sentence below.

3.

Circle/highlight the word *therefore* in verse 13. This word indicates a shift that begins in verse 13. Reread verses 13–25. Summarize Peter's main message to the exiles in these verses in one sentence below.

LET'S TAKE A CLOSER LOOK...

1.

Beginning in verse 13, Peter gives clear instructions to the exiles on how to live faithfully. Fill in column two of the chart below with each instruction. If Peter includes a why or how, make note of that in column three.

Verses	Instruction	Why/How?	Application
13	Set your hope fully on the grace of Jesus Christ	Preparing your minds for action and being sober-minded	Pay attention to the thoughts I am allowing into my mind today and set them back on Jesus
14			
15			
17–19			
22–23			

2.

Reflect on how you could practically apply each of these instructions in your own life. Make note of these practical applications in column four.

3. _____

Look at all the places you marked *Jesus* in chapter 1. List below what Peter reminds us about *who* Jesus is and what He *has done* for us.

4. _____

Refer back to the summary sentences you wrote at the beginning of this chapter. What is the significance of the order of Peter's messaging? Why does he begin with the message of verses 1–12 and then follow it with the message of verses 13–25 versus the other way around?

5. _____

What does this insight from Peter show us about *how* and *why* we can live faithfully?

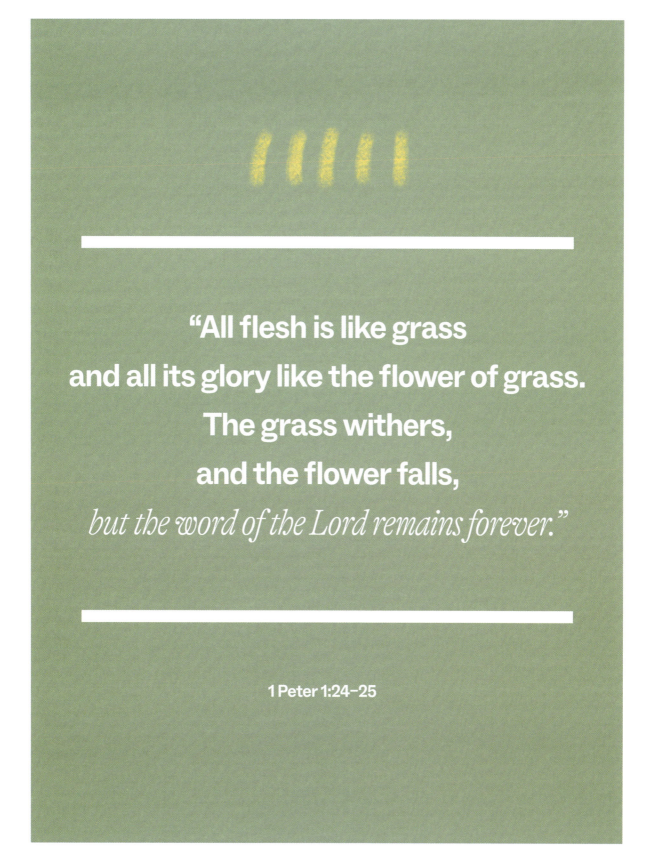

"All flesh is like grass
and all its glory like the flower of grass.
The grass withers,
and the flower falls,
but the word of the Lord remains forever."

1 Peter 1:24–25

Go to God *in Prayer.*

Before we move on to the second chapter of 1 Peter, take a moment to bring all you have learned in chapter 1 before Jesus. Thank Him for all He has done for you. What does it feel like knowing that He did all these things for *you?* Out of love for *you?* Lay your heart out before Him and write your prayer to Him below.

CHAPTER FOURTEEN

Faithful Living as Exiles

1 Peter 2

> We will continue today with the second chapter of Peter's first letter.

Let's begin with observation.

Read 1 Peter chapter 2 and underline any descriptive names or phrases Peter uses to refer to the exiles (the letter's recipients). *(For example, newborn infants, living stones, etc.)*

1 Peter 2

1. So put away all malice and all deceit and hypocrisy and envy and all slander.
2. Like newborn infants, long for the pure spiritual milk, that by it you may grow up into salvation—
3. if indeed you have tasted that the Lord is good.
4. As you come to him, a living stone rejected by men but in the sight of God chosen and precious,
5. you yourselves like living stones are being built up as a spiritual house, to be a holy priesthood, to offer spiritual sacrifices acceptable to God through Jesus Christ.
6. For it stands in Scripture:

    "Behold, I am laying in Zion a stone,
    a cornerstone chosen and precious,
    and whoever believes in him will not be put to shame."

7. So the honor is for you who believe, but for those who do not believe,

    "The stone that the builders rejected
    has become the cornerstone,"

8. and

    "A stone of stumbling,
    and a rock of offense."

    They stumble because they disobey the word, as they were destined to do.
9. But you are a chosen race, a royal priesthood, a holy nation, a people for his own possession, that you may proclaim the excellencies of him who called you out of darkness into his marvelous light.
10. Once you were not a people, but now you are God's people; once you had not received mercy, but now you have received mercy.
11. Beloved, I urge you as sojourners and exiles to abstain from the passions of the flesh, which wage war against your soul.

SCRIPTURE

12 Keep your conduct among the Gentiles honorable, so that when they speak against you as evildoers, they may see your good deeds and glorify God on the day of visitation.

13 Be subject for the Lord's sake to every human institution, whether it be to the emperor as supreme,

14 or to governors as sent by him to punish those who do evil and to praise those who do good.

15 For this is the will of God, that by doing good you should put to silence the ignorance of foolish people.

16 Live as people who are free, not using your freedom as a cover-up for evil, but living as servants of God.

17 Honor everyone. Love the brotherhood. Fear God. Honor the emperor.

18 Servants, be subject to your masters with all respect, not only to the good and gentle but also to the unjust.

19 For this is a gracious thing, when, mindful of God, one endures sorrows while suffering unjustly.

20 For what credit is it if, when you sin and are beaten for it, you endure? But if when you do good and suffer for it you endure, this is a gracious thing in the sight of God.

21 For to this you have been called, because Christ also suffered for you, leaving you an example, so that you might follow in his steps.

22 He committed no sin, neither was deceit found in his mouth.

23 When he was reviled, he did not revile in return; when he suffered, he did not threaten, but continued entrusting himself to him who judges justly.

24 He himself bore our sins in his body on the tree, that we might die to sin and live to righteousness. By his wounds you have been healed.

25 For you were straying like sheep, but have now returned to the Shepherd and Overseer of your souls.

LET'S TAKE A CLOSER LOOK...

1. _____

Write these descriptive names or phrases in column two of the chart below, according to the verses in which they appear. If multiple names appear in a single verse, list them all. Include any further description that Peter gives for each name in column three.

Verse	Name	Description
2	Newborn infants	Longing for pure spiritual milk to grow up in salvation
5		
9		
10		

FAITHFUL LIVING, PART ONE

2.

Peter continues his instructions for the exiles in chapter 2. Fill in column two of the chart below with each instruction. If Peter includes a why or how, make note of that in column three.

Verses	Instruction	Why/How?	Application
11	Abstain from the passions of the flesh	Because they wage war against our souls being sober-minded	Pray for the person I am feeling animosity towards
12			
13–15			
16			
17			
18–19			

3. ─────────

Again, think about how you could practically apply each of these instructions to your own life. Make note of these practical applications in column four.

Note: While Peter's instructions refer to submitting to human authority, elsewhere in Scripture we are only to do so insofar as it is not disobeying God (see Acts 5:12–42; Romans 13:1–2; 1 Peter 4:14–16).

SUBMITTING TO AUTHORITY

Scan the QR code to learn more about our guidelines in Scripture.

Go to God *in Prayer.*

We hope that you have seen throughout this study that faithful living is more about a change in heart and perspective than it is about a checklist of behaviors. With that being said, the practicality of Peter's instructions can be helpful for our own lives.

Look back through Peter's instructions to the exiles from both chapters and your applications. Take time to slow down and talk with God about which of Peter's instructions strike a chord with you.

Which of your discoveries is God asking you to apply on a deeper level, even starting today? Invite Him to help you. Write your prayer to Him below.

CHAPTER FIFTEEN

Joy in Suffering

1 Peter 1–2

Taking a closer look at key words in the biblical text helps us to slow down and notice emerging patterns. Let's review 1 Peter 1–2 and look for key words.

Let's begin with observation.

Marking key words in the Bible helps us to slow down and notice patterns and themes that emerge in the text. Read through 1 Peter 1–2 once more and mark each of these words with a different color or symbol:

- *Jesus* and synonyms and pronouns for Him (Note: You have already done this for chapter one.)

- *Suffering/trials* and synonyms

- *Rejoice/joy* and synonyms

Here are some marking suggestions:

1. "... through the resurrection of Jesus Christ..."

2. "... when he predicted the sufferings of Christ..."

3. "In this you rejoice..."

1 Peter 1

1. Peter, an apostle of Jesus Christ,

    To those who are elect exiles of the Dispersion in Pontus, Galatia, Cappadocia, Asia, and Bithynia,

2. according to the foreknowledge of God the Father, in the sanctification of the Spirit, for obedience to Jesus Christ and for sprinkling with his blood: May grace and peace be multiplied to you.

3. Blessed be the God and Father of our Lord Jesus Christ! According to his great mercy, he has caused us to be born again to a living hope through the resurrection of Jesus Christ from the dead,

4. to an inheritance that is imperishable, undefiled, and unfading, kept in heaven for you,

5. who by God's power are being guarded through faith for a salvation ready to be revealed in the last time.

6. In this you rejoice, though now for a little while, if necessary, you have been grieved by various trials,

7. so that the tested genuineness of your faith—more precious than gold that perishes though it is tested by fire—may be found to result in praise and glory and honor at the revelation of Jesus Christ.

8. Though you have not seen him, you love him. Though you do not now see him, you believe in him and rejoice with joy that is inexpressible and filled with glory,

9. obtaining the outcome of your faith, the salvation of your souls.

10. Concerning this salvation, the prophets who prophesied about the grace that was to be yours searched and inquired carefully,

11. inquiring what person or time the Spirit of Christ in them was indicating when he predicted the sufferings of Christ and the subsequent glories.

12. It was revealed to them that they were serving not themselves but you, in the things that have now been announced to you through those who preached the good news to you by the Holy Spirit sent from heaven, things into which angels long to look.

SCRIPTURE

13 Therefore, preparing your minds for action, and being sober-minded, set your hope fully on the grace that will be brought to you at the revelation of Jesus Christ.
14 As obedient children, do not be conformed to the passions of your former ignorance,
15 but as he who called you is holy, you also be holy in all your conduct,
16 since it is written, "You shall be holy, for I am holy."
17 And if you call on him as Father who judges impartially according to each one's deeds, conduct yourselves with fear throughout the time of your exile,
18 knowing that you were ransomed from the futile ways inherited from your forefathers, not with perishable things such as silver or gold,
19 but with the precious blood of Christ, like that of a lamb without blemish or spot.
20 He was foreknown before the foundation of the world but was made manifest in the last times for the sake of you
21 who through him are believers in God, who raised him from the dead and gave him glory, so that your faith and hope are in God.
22 Having purified your souls by your obedience to the truth for a sincere brotherly love, love one another earnestly from a pure heart,
23 since you have been born again, not of perishable seed but of imperishable, through the living and abiding word of God;
24 for
"All flesh is like grass
and all its glory like the flower of grass.
The grass withers,
and the flower falls,
25 but the word of the Lord remains forever."
And this word is the good news that was preached to you.

1 Peter 2

1. So put away all malice and all deceit and hypocrisy and envy and all slander.
2. Like newborn infants, long for the pure spiritual milk, that by it you may grow up into salvation—
3. if indeed you have tasted that the Lord is good.
4. As you come to him, a living stone rejected by men but in the sight of God chosen and precious,
5. you yourselves like living stones are being built up as a spiritual house, to be a holy priesthood, to offer spiritual sacrifices acceptable to God through Jesus Christ.
6. For it stands in Scripture:

    "Behold, I am laying in Zion a stone,
    a cornerstone chosen and precious,
    and whoever believes in him will not be put to shame."

7. So the honor is for you who believe, but for those who do not believe,

    "The stone that the builders rejected
    has become the cornerstone,"

8. and

    "A stone of stumbling,
    and a rock of offense."

    They stumble because they disobey the word, as they were destined to do.
9. But you are a chosen race, a royal priesthood, a holy nation, a people for his own possession, that you may proclaim the excellencies of him who called you out of darkness into his marvelous light.
10. Once you were not a people, but now you are God's people; once you had not received mercy, but now you have received mercy.
11. Beloved, I urge you as sojourners and exiles to abstain from the passions of the flesh, which wage war against your soul.

SCRIPTURE

12 Keep your conduct among the Gentiles honorable, so that when they speak against you as evildoers, they may see your good deeds and glorify God on the day of visitation.
13 Be subject for the Lord's sake to every human institution, whether it be to the emperor as supreme,
14 or to governors as sent by him to punish those who do evil and to praise those who do good.
15 For this is the will of God, that by doing good you should put to silence the ignorance of foolish people.
16 Live as people who are free, not using your freedom as a cover-up for evil, but living as servants of God.
17 Honor everyone. Love the brotherhood. Fear God. Honor the emperor.
18 Servants, be subject to your masters with all respect, not only to the good and gentle but also to the unjust.
19 For this is a gracious thing, when, mindful of God, one endures sorrows while suffering unjustly.
20 For what credit is it if, when you sin and are beaten for it, you endure? But if when you do good and suffer for it you endure, this is a gracious thing in the sight of God.
21 For to this you have been called, because Christ also suffered for you, leaving you an example, so that you might follow in his steps.
22 He committed no sin, neither was deceit found in his mouth.
23 When he was reviled, he did not revile in return; when he suffered, he did not threaten, but continued entrusting himself to him who judges justly.
24 He himself bore our sins in his body on the tree, that we might die to sin and live to righteousness. By his wounds you have been healed.
25 For you were straying like sheep, but have now returned to the Shepherd and Overseer of your souls.

LET'S TAKE A CLOSER LOOK...

One of the words we marked, and one of the themes of Peter's message in chapters 1–2, is *suffering.* For context, Peter was writing to exiles facing significant persecution from the Roman government for their faith in Jesus.

1.

What does Peter teach the exiles about suffering, particularly in 1:6-7 and 2:20-21?

2.

Look to where you marked rejoice/joy in these chapters. How does suffering connect to rejoicing?

3.

How does suffering connect us to Jesus?

4.

Suffering is a part of life, and navigating our personal pain is a part of faithful living. Take a moment to think back on past trials you have walked through. How have you personally experienced the truth of Peter's words?

5.

How can Peter's teachings and instructions encourage you in any suffering you may be walking through or may walk through in the future?

SUFFERING

Scan the QR code to discover more about how these truths apply to our lives.

Go to God *in Prayer.*

If there are any current sufferings in your life, in the life of someone you love, or in the world around you that are weighing heavy on you, take a moment to lay them down before Jesus. He understands, and He cares for you. Be honest with Jesus about what is on your heart, including anything that feels hard, confusing, or sad right now. Ask Him to help you carry the burden. Surrender it all to Him. Remind Him, and your own heart, of what Scripture says about who He is and what He has done for you. And because of that, you can walk through suffering in His presence and strength. Write your prayer to Him below. He is listening. And He loves you.

Take a step *in community.*

After you have laid these burdens down at the feet of Jesus, take an opportunity to *talk with someone else.* Share what is on your heart. Ask them to pray with you and for you. This is the gift of community.

> Not sure what to say? You can start like this:
>
> *I am working through a Bible Study on faithful living, and I have been learning about suffering. I have some painful things happening in my own life. Would you be willing to help me process some of these things and pray with me?*

CONNECTION IN COMMUNITY

Scan the QR code to listen to a roundtable discussion on living faithfully as an exile.

CHAPTER SIXTEEN

Summary

1 Peter 1–2

Spend time slowing down and reflecting on all you have discovered from 1 Peter 1–2 by filling out the summary chart on the next page.

If there are some questions that you are unable to answer today, that's okay. We will practice this at the end of each passage of Scripture. A question that is hard today may become clearer as you go on. At the end of the study, we will look at all the charts together to see the Bible as one full story and how our own stories intersect with God's story.

1 PETER 1-2 SUMMARY CHART

Theme/Big Idea

What did you learn about God/Jesus?

What did you learn about yourself?

What did you learn about living in exile?

What did you learn about faithful living?

Personal Takeaway

love
one another
earnestly from
a *pure heart*

1 Peter 1:22

Go to God *in Prayer.*

Bring all your sufferings, joys, and hopes to God in prayer. Thank Him for all that He has taught you and revealed to you through Scripture in 1 Peter 1–2. Thank Him for walking with you through this journey. As we near the end of this study, share with Him all that is on your mind and in your heart. Share with Him what you need and your hopes. Write your prayer to Him below.

CHAPTER SEVENTEEN

Wrap-Up

How It Fits Together

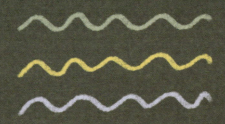

Over the past two weeks, we have journeyed through the Bible in pursuit of faithful living—through Genesis, Hebrews, Nehemiah, Jeremiah, and 1 Peter. As we wrap up this study, let's take a step back and retrace the thread we have been following. Our goal is to understand the Bible as one full story, seeing how it fits together and how our own stories intersect with God's story. Take time to review each of the summary charts that you have filled out.

Genesis 3	Page 42
Hebrews 11	Page 68
Nehemiah 1–2	Page 100
Jeremiah 29	Page 128
1 Peter 1–2	Page 170

Compare and contrast them to each other to see the full picture of living as exiles with a heart turned toward heaven throughout Scripture. When you are finished, take time to reflect on and answer the following questions.

LET'S REFLECT...

1.

Together, we have traced this theme of faithful living as exiles and have seen it unfold through different parts of Scripture. Has this affected your perspective on the Bible as one whole, complete story? If so, how?

2.

How did your understanding of yourself as an exile grow throughout the study?

3.

How did your understanding of faithful living grow?

4.

What are the biggest takeaways or truths that you want to remember and carry with you from this study?

Go to God *in Prayer.*

Take a moment to come before God and thank Him for being the author of our stories from the beginning of time until now. Share your heart and feelings with Him. Ask Him to help you meditate on the truths you have discovered throughout this study. Invite Him into the rest of your day. Write your prayer to Him below.

CHAPTER EIGHTEEN

Self-Reflection #3

As we close our time in this study, let's take a moment to pause and reflect on our journey.

We traced the thread of exiles through the Bible—from Adam and Eve in Genesis to the faithful men and women of Hebrews 11, from Nehemiah and Jeremiah to the Christian exiles that lived in the first century. We recognized ourselves as exiles in a world that is not our home. And through the example of many of these men and women, we learned what faithful living looks like here and now, even as we await our heavenly homecoming.

Self-Reflection #3

Before we close, let's take a moment to reflect on the work God has begun in and through us.

1. After following the thread of exiles and faithful living throughout the Bible, where do you see your story intersecting with God's story?

2. Look back on your initial prayer with God on page 38. Can you see a difference in your thoughts, perspectives, heart, or actions since you've begun? Explain your answer.

3. In what ways do you hope to continue to pursue seeing the world through the eyes of God?

Go to God *in Prayer.*

After you have self-reflected, spend time with God. Give Him thanks and glory for this journey we have been on together. Praise Him for the work He has begun in and through you. Thank Him for the truths you have discovered through Scripture. Ask Him for whatever you need to continue your pursuit of living with a heart turned toward heaven.

Letter to the Reader

Thank you for persevering to the end of this study! You have made sacrifices, overcome struggles, and chosen to come back day after day to sit with the Lord and deepen your relationship with Him. You showed up. And you kept showing up. There is truly nothing more important than that.

If life still feels messy, if you still have questions, if faithful living still feels hard, that's okay. Life will continue to be messy, confusing, and hard as long as we are exiles on this side of eternity. You aren't meant to have faithful living figured out because you've finished Part One of this study.

We do hope, though, that you now have some tools and truths to lean on and come back to as you continue your lifelong pursuit of living with a heart turned toward heaven. We hope you have found some community through this process and know that you do not have to do it alone. Most importantly, we pray you have encountered the heart of Jesus, who has been with you all along and will continue to be with you, from now until forever. We are praying alongside you on your journey as well!

God's grace abounds for you. You are loved.

A Prayer for Faithful Living

Father,

As I travel this earth as an exile,
Grant me eyes to see this world as You do.

Grant me a mind that is attuned to heaven.

Grant me a heart that longs for my true home.

Grant me hands to love and serve my city and my neighbor,
here and now.

Grant me feet that will follow You wherever You may lead.

Grant me the grace to live faithfully,

For You and Your glory.

Amen.

WAY TO GO!

We'd love to congratulate you personally! Scan the QR code for a video of encouragement from a Yarrow team member!

We hope you have enjoyed this Yarrow Bible study guide.

Continue your journey into understanding faithful living as an exile with the complete Faithful Living Series.

Sojourn:
Flourishing on Earth, Yearning for Heaven
Faithful Living, Part One

Purpose:
Eternal Significance in Everyday Work
Faithful Living, Part Two

Together:
Union with Christ and Each Other
Faithful Living, Part Three

Anchored:
Finding Peace in an Anxious World
Faithful Living, Part Four

Conviction:
Loving Well, Living Differently
Faithful Living, Part Five

For these and other Yarrow Bible Studies, visit Yarrow.org.